A WALK
WITH
FATHER

• • • • • • • • • •

Sharing My Story,
Singing My Song

JUDY MENDEZ MARTINEZ

A WALK WITH FATHER: SHARING MY STORY,
SINGING MY SONG
Copyright © 2021 by Judy Mendez Martinez
ISBN 978-1-7345235-7-7

Designed & Published by King's Daughter Publishing
Indian Trail, North Carolina 28079
www.KingsDaughterPublishing.com

Cover Art, "Snow Play–Dad & Daughter" by Vicki Wade.
Used by permssion.

Printed in the United States of America.

Table of Contents

● ● ● ● ● ● ● ● ● ● ●

Acknowledgements

● ● ● ● ● ● ● ● ● ● ● ●

To the man that is the wind beneath my wings, my husband Edwin. My biggest fan and encourager. Thank you for always believing in me and seeing me in a way I had not been able to.

To my prayer team and their prayers. To my sister Reina who has always told me, "You can do it."

To my beautiful Girls, Yvette and Jenny, it was because of you I kept going.

To S. Kristi Douglas for supporting me and encouraging me to move forward.

Thank you to Tito Atiles for being instrumental in opening the door to Cristo Viene ministries that paved the way to other opportunities.

To my sister Carmen for being my great partner and inspiration.

To David Quinones, Trio Melodico Congregacional, Mickey Melendez, Millie, Minerva, and the musicians who were always so willing to help by providing background vocals and great music for my recordings.

To Pastor Anibal Mercado for being the first one to give me the opportunity to use my writing, acting and directing skills within his church ministry. To Gilberto and Mari for always encouraging me. To every pastor who said, "yes."

To my wonderful, blessed, awesome Father God who chose me, called me out and gifted me to share from my heart my songs, writing and directing gifts.

Thank you.

~ Judy Mendez Martinez

Foreword

My wife Maritza and I had the privilege of meeting Judy and her husband Edwin in 2001. As I got to know Judy, I witnessed her heart for community and how she enjoyed people. This was evident very quickly and I was impressed with her gifting in song and musical ministry.

She has a great passion for theater (acting/comedy/musicals) but what really impressed me—and still does—is her humility. We enjoyed great fellowship and she shared her experience serving the *Cristo Viene* Ministry with the beloved Founder and Evangelist, Yiye Avila, who was like the Billy Graham of Latin America.

Judy draws us in as she speaks from the heart recounting many of her life events and how, through faith in God, she was able to see a great turn around as He intervened on her behalf. As you read through this anecdotal writing of her life experiences in the Lord, you will see how you too can enjoy a walk with the Father, daily. This book, A Walk with Father, is a picture of His love and care for His children. It as an honor to write this forward. I know this book will bless you as much as it has blessed me.

~ Pastor Gilberto Colón
Gilberto Colón Ministries

Chapter 1: Starting Over

• • ● • ● • ● • ● • ● • ● • ●

"The God who made us also can remake us."
~ Woodrow Kroll

*E*VERY MORNING WHEN THE SUN RISES AND BY GOD'S GRACE BRINGS A NEW DAY TO US, WE ARE BLESSED. Every day we are afforded an opportunity for growth and change. In many cases, we can begin a new chapter—something new to write for that day's history. It's an opportunity to evaluate our lives and choose a new road if the one we are on is heading in the wrong direction.

Change is hard when you are on the road of addiction. Addiction is not something you can just turn off unless by God's grace He gives you the strength to do it. Life with a family member struggling with addiction is heart-wrenching. It's very painful to see the toll addiction takes on a person you love. Such was the case with my father.

He was a good man that was caught in the web of addiction. On weekends, our apartment was the place for friends and family to come and party. Smoke clouds filled our living room. Alcohol flowed freely as loud music played in the background. Partygoers drank until they didn't know who they were, where they were or what they were doing.

One such evening when it was time for the party to end, my dad offered to walk my uncle to his apartment. Once they got there, my uncle insisted on walking my father back to his apartment so that he wouldn't walk alone. Each insisted on walking the other back and forth like this for several hours until they passed out. Like clockwork, every weekend the party was on. I was very young, maybe about five, when I would stand and watch as they smoked, drank, and danced the night away. It looked more like a tavern than a home. I remember men picking me up to dance. They swung me around as my feet flung in the air. When no one was looking, I would chug the little bit of beer left in the beer cans on the table. I don't recall ever seeing my mother drunk but she sat there and smoked a pack of cigarettes in minutes. She even put some of the ashes on her tongue.

I don't know if it was the anger of being addicted that caused my father to cut himself on his arms with blades, but he did it often. When Dad was drunk—which was often—my siblings and I became afraid. There were times where he threw plates around or fought with Mom. I remember these scenes from the age of five, but it had been going on many years before that. We hid, we cried and in our innocence we prayed. God hears prayers even when the one praying doesn't even know He really exists.

A WALK WITH FATHER

My oldest brother, Octavio, was riding his bike one day when he happened to hear music coming from a church called Chicago Tabernacle on Clark and Halstead. He was curious to see what was going on so he got off his bike and stood in front of the door. A gentleman sitting on the back row near the door noticed him and asked him to come in, but his insistence only made Octavio take off. Every time he rode his bike, he would stop in front of the church to listen. God had a purpose in this.

One day, Octavio stopped in front of the church again and watched a special program that piqued his interest so he stood there for quite a while. As he was intently watching, the same gentleman invited him in. When my brother refused, he asked him where he lived. My brother, fearing what our mother would say, did not answer and took off. The man followed him home but did not come in. However, one day he just showed up! He introduced himself as Clarence Hiltunen. Clarence had been a faithful member of the church who by God's inspiration had made our family his mission. He had seen something in my brother, a yearning, a sadness, or perhaps a prayer needing to be answered.

Once at the door, he asked if he could come in, but my mother (who did not speak or understand English) refused to let him in. Besides, she said to us later, "I don't need his church or his God." But when God sets something in motion in answer to prayer, nothing will stop it. Clarence insisted on coming and the next time he did, he brought an interpreter. Because my brother kept stopping by the church and returned home with Clarence, Mom became very curious and decided to see why my brother kept going back. She went once alone then again with my father but because the language barrier made it hard for her to understand anything, she didn't go back. Dad continued visiting the church and Clarence continued to visit our home.

The day came when Dad gave his life to the Lord and our family saw, little by little, the changes this brought. Eventually, the parties stopped and instead of offering parties and alcohol, our dad offered what he had found, Jesus. Friends and family said he'd lost his mind and stopped coming around. Some didn't even speak to him anymore, but he kept going forward with his faith. It took our mother a little longer to come but eventually she, too, joined us. All this happened because one night some children hiding, crying and afraid asked God to change their father.

It was God who directed my brother to the Chicago Tabernacle church. It was God who put the persistence in Clarence's heart to pursue a family crying out for help. It was an answer to our prayer. Isn't that just like God?

The year was 1959 when my dad turned his life around. Both he and Mom changed completely and remained faithful to their change, to their faith, until the day they died. My mother went on to study at the Spanish Bible Institute and became a teacher at the church. Years later, she became an associate pastor at the church she and our brother-in-law, Miguel, started. They were both very loved by the church members. Years later, when we were grown, Dad would look at us and cry, "I almost destroyed my beautiful family." He was so grateful how God had turned his life around and how all his children were serving the Lord. When Mom passed, the funeral hall was so full, not one more person could enter. There were hundreds of people paying their respects to a woman who had touched so many lives. Dad's funeral also had many people in attendance. There were many witnesses of the beautiful change God had made in their lives.

I didn't go into full detail of all the things our family endured when our parents were living a life ignorant of God and His great mercy, but the important thing is that when prayers were lifted, God stepped in and saved our family.

Do you need a restart to your life? Or is that your prayer for someone you love? The God who rescued our family all those years ago can do the same for you. There are count-less stories of lives that have been turned around by the grace of God. There is nothing you have done that God can't turn around. No one is out of his reach. As Betsie ten Boom once said, "There is no pit too deep that God isn't deeper still."

Addiction is not something that can be turned on and off. For some, it takes years of counseling and intervention. I offer you a way—the way I saw my dad and others take to be set free.

Every morning you wake, remember it's a day to start

over. It's a new opportunity for change. If you can't do it on your own, call out to God. He is the same yesterday, today and tomorrow. God has not lost His power to transform those who call on Him. We do our part by acknowledging God. He does His part by transforming us.

If you are struggling with addiction of any kind, I offer this prayer for you.

Dear Heavenly Father,

I pray for the person reading this right now. I come to You as someone who has witnessed firsthand the change that comes from trusting our lives to You. There is no addiction, no chain, no power that is holding them that Your power and Your love can't cut through and destroy. Take away the desire to go after the addiction that holds them bound and restore the years this addiction has stolen from them and their family. You are the restorer of our souls as your word says in Psalm 23. I pray You restore their soul. Guide them along the right path; that path that leads to You. I pray You would remove every barrier that keeps them from receiving the miracle of freedom that comes from trusting their lives to You. I pray that when the voice of temptation speaks to them, it fall on deaf ears; that their ears would be open to hear the voice of the Good Shepherd. I declare that as they make this prayer their own, the scales would fall from their eyes and they will see clearly the lies this addiction has made them see as real, as a way of escape from their fears, insecurities and lack. I ask that You turn their mourning into dancing; that the old things pass away and You create a new thing in their life. I declare the former things that kept them bound will cease and desist from whispering deception in their ears. Your word declares You to be the same yesterday, today and tomorrow. What You did for my family yesterday, You can certainly do today for theirs. Oh God, keep them from the devourer of their soul. Let them see their way clear to You. Restore their life, their marriage, and their family I pray in Jesus' name. Be glorified. Oh Lord, be glorified.

Pray, trust, receive.

Chapter 2:
Picture of God

• • • • • • • • • • • • • •

"But God, being rich in mercy, because of the great love with
which he loved us, even when we were dead in our trespasses,
made us alive together with Christ—
by grace you have been saved."
~ Eph 2:4-5 (NIV)

WHAT PICTURE DO YOU HAVE OF GOD? Do you see Him sitting on a throne with white hair and a white beard looking down on earth ready to fling fiery thunder on anyone whom He finds displeasing?

There's an old adage that says, "A picture is worth a thousand words." Pictures are a powerful tool in that they engrain themselves in our minds. Have you ever heard someone say, "I can't unsee that?" That's because pictures, even those in your mind, are just as powerful. When you read a story, your mind starts seeing what is being read, as if in moving pictures. The more you imagine it, the more real it becomes.

A picture shows us what a person looks like—the color of the eyes, skin and hair. It shows us the shape of the face, nose and chin. If we look at a picture of someone we haven't met but we look at the image long enough, when we meet the person, we might feel as if we knew them all along. Spoken words become pictures when they are heard repeatedly. It's what you see in your mind's eye, especially when you are a child.

When I was younger, I had a distorted picture of God. I started going to church with my parents when I was just six years old. We went to a small "fire-breathing" church. The men who stood on the platform walked back and forth spitting their fiery sermons; hitting with their fists on the pulpit as they painted a picture of an angry God. "Why were these men so angry?" I wondered. I sat there wide-eyed with my head going back and forth as they flounced across the platform. I imagined God looking down at me ready to pounce. In all honesty, I was afraid of God. Sure, there were sermons about the love of God but those messages were few and far between. They usually ended with, "Don't forget, God is love but He is also a consuming fiya!!!"

I felt quite sad because I wanted to be good. I didn't want to make God mad or offend Him in any way, but I never felt like I could ever measure up. It's impossible to please an angry God and that's the picture I carried for many years. In no way, shape or form am I trying to malign the church. To the contrary, I am so thankful that my parents' lives were turned around completely when they accepted the life Jesus Christ gives. However, as a child, it was very hard for me to understand many things.

When I was 14 years old, there was a boy who liked me. One day, my sister-in-law took us to the park. I was walking ahead of them. Suddenly he called my name. When I turned around, he planted a kiss on my lips. I was shocked and scared. I got so nervous I fell to the ground! Then I got up and ran as fast as I could. I imagined for sure God was going to open up the ground and swallow me! The boy was dumbfounded but I bet it did a lot for his ego. He probably thought he was a Romeo.

I remember as young as 16 going into days of fasting because I so wanted to please God but like Paul, I fell short. Paul wrote in Romans 7:15, *"I don't really understand myself, for I want to do what is right, but I don't do it. Instead, I do what I hate."* Who was going to free me from myself? You might wonder what a girl of 16 was doing to feel as I did, but when your picture of God is distorted, anything can seem like a great sin, including what I thought, what I wanted and things I did.

Something as simple as not feeling like praying, not reading the Bible enough, or wanting to go places the church considered sinful made me feel guilty. The picture presented was so bad that for years I was even afraid to laugh because I was told, *"¡Cuidado que risa para en llanto!"* In English, "Be careful, too much laughter ends in weeping!" Not everyone perceives things the same way or has the same reaction, but I was a very impressionable child and took so many things literally.

I once read a fable by Aesop called, "The Wind and

the Sun." In this fable, the North Wind boasted of great strength. The Sun argued, "There is great power in gentleness. We shall have a contest." Far below, a man traveled a winding road. He was wearing a warm winter coat. "As a test of strength," said The Sun, "let us see which of us can take the coat off of that man." "It will be quite simple for me to force him to remove his coat," bragged The Wind. The Wind blew so hard, the birds clung to the trees. The world was filled with dust and leaves. But the harder The Wind blew down the road, the tighter the shivering man clung to his coat. Then, The Sun came out from behind a cloud. The Sun warmed the air and the frosty ground. The man on the road unbuttoned his coat. The Sun grew slowly brighter and brighter. Soon the man felt so hot, he took off his coat and sat down in a shady spot. "How did you do that?" asked The Wind. "It was easy," said The Sun, "I lit the day. Through gentleness I got my way."

God has been showing us His love from the beginning of creation. In fact, 1 John 4:19 says, *"We love because He first loved us"* (NIV). He doesn't come to us with force but with His gentle love. *"See what great love the Father has lavished on us, that we should be called children of God! And that is what we are"* (1 Jn 3:1a NIV).

I was seeing an incomplete picture of God. I was just a seeing a negative. That is what was impressed, sealed, and locked into my mind for many years. I know there were others who felt the same way. Some fell away because they just couldn't handle the guilt. Those preachers painted the picture they saw. Perhaps it was a picture presented to them. It was very unfortunate because I wasted so many years not fully being able to let loose and let God use me to the extent He wanted to. I held myself back because I felt I couldn't please Him enough.

I am so thankful to a loving God who through the years has shown me that He is a God of love and great mercy; a God who says He forgives our sins and remembers them no more (Heb 8:12). I finally accepted the fact that no matter how "good" I was, it wasn't at all about me! I learned that I could never be justified by my own doing or good works but by the work of Jesus for me (Rom 3:24).

It wasn't meant for me to reach God, heaven and salvation by my own strength. I needed to trust that what Jesus did on the cross of Calvary was enough to save me and bring me to Him. Ephesians 2:8-9 reads, *"For it is by grace you have been saved, through faith—and this is not from yourselves, it is the gift of God—not by works, so that no one can boast"* (NIV).

In my picture, I was the giver and God was the receiver! Paul writes in Philippians 2:13, *"For it is God who works in you to will and to act in order to fulfill his good purpose"* (NIV). God through Jesus laid the way for our salvation.

As we grow, learn, and seek Him ourselves, the picture starts to change. As I began to read scripture and listen to the full message of salvation and God's redemptive power, the full picture of a loving God came into view. Before, I was seeing a negative of God just like the negative of a photograph.

Today, most photographers use digital photography to bring pictures into view. Before digital photography however, film was developed in a special room, a dark room. There was a special process they used in order to bring about a clear picture of their subject. It was a process that required certain tools and special light-sensitive photographic paper that would keep the photograph from over-processing. Once the photograph was fully developed, the image was ready to be seen and enjoyed. Before, I was seeing a negative of God just like the negative of a photograph. It wasn't quite developed. I wasn't getting to see Him fully. But as I searched the scriptures, the picture became clearer. I was able to focus on it now in a new light. I was able to see God as my heavenly father who loved me and desired fellowship with me.

How could we think that our love is stronger than God's? When our children disappoint or do something that really upsets us, do we walk away? Do we punish them to the point of death? Do we condemn them to a loveless life? No! No parent in their right mind would do such a thing. We love our children and even when they break our hearts, we listen to them. We care about what hurts them. We want to help them even at times when we know they need to go through tough times in order for them to learn and grow. How then can we think any differently of God?

Matthew 7:9-11 says, "*Which of you, if your son asks for bread, will give him a stone? Or if he asks for a fish, will give him a snake? If you, then, though you are evil, know how to give good gifts to your children, how much more will your Father in heaven give good gifts to those who ask Him"* (NIV).

God is love and He painted the greatest picture ever— Jesus on the cross of Calvary with arms open wide to all who would come. Through Jesus, the price has been paid— the price we could never pay. Isn't that awesome? Doesn't that give a sense of relief?

Then what about the picture of God? You know, the angry one? Well, if you read the Bible you will see that God's wrath came on the children of disobedience, in other words, those who willfully and purposefully sinned. In the Old Testament, there are many passages that show where God punished Israel (see Isa 48). The consequence of their stubbornness was punishment. When they truly humbled themselves before the Lord, He always forgave them and rescued them. Even though they were very stouthearted and willfully sinful, God loved them. In Zechariah 2:8, God calls them the apple of His eye! God's very nature is love but He is also a holy God and will not tolerate willful sin.

We can't see half of the picture though. There is a day of judgment appointed for all mankind where all will receive what is due them, whether good or bad (see 1 Cor 5:10 and Jn 3:18). We have all been given a choice to choose love or wrath, but wrath is not what God offers. It's not what He created us for. Sometimes we insist on doing our own thing our own way, completely disregarding Him. God loves us so much He let us know in His word what things will keep us apart from him. He doesn't depart from man; man chooses to depart from him.

Just as a parent lays down the rules, so does God. Unfortunately, the only picture some have of God, is the one presented to them—a God of wrath and consuming fire, not of a loving father who is eager to forgive. They leave out the beauty and wonder of the saving grace and love of God. Ephesians 2:4-6 reads, *"But because of His great love for us, God, who is rich in mercy, made us alive with Christ even when we were dead in transgressions—it is by grace you have been saved. And God raised us up with Christ and seated us with Him in the heavenly realms in Christ Jesus"* (NIV).

Jesus is the perfect picture of redeeming grace (see Jn 4 and 8). There are consequences to our choices, but God is ready to let you see the picture of His love and forgiveness. You are never so far gone that the love of God can't reach you. He understands our human frailties and our propensity to sin. Ever since Adam and Eve reached for sin and disobedience, mankind has followed suit. Day after day, year after year, century after century, God has never gone back on His word. He can't. He is not man that He should lie or change his mind and He always does what He says (Num 23:19).

No parent wants their child to feel forced to love them. Neither does God. God doesn't want you to come because you are afraid or feel like you have no choice. He wants you to come because He loves you. He says to you today, *"Come to me, all you who are weary and burdened, and I will give you rest*" (Matt 11:28 NIV).

He offers rest from trying to do it on your own. Rest from staring at the wrong picture. Turn that negative into a positive, trust God with your life and you will see the beauty He offers you. Don't let the picture you are storing in your heart keep you from experiencing love unending.

Chapter 3:
If She'd Only Turn Around

● ● ● ● ● ● ● ● ● ● ● ● ● ●

*"There's no way to be a perfect mother and
a million ways to be a good one."*
—Jill Churchill

I REMEMBER AS A CHILD ALWAYS WANTING TO BE NEAR MY MOTHER. It didn't matter where she went in the house, my eyes followed her as she went from room to room busily doing her daily chores. Most of the time, however, she was in the kitchen. On many occasions, I would sit on the floor just outside the kitchen where I could see her while I did my scribble art on a notepad.

I would look at her with longing eyes as she stirred the rice, cut potatoes and diced some onions. She went from the refrigerator to the stove, then to the sink and back to the stove almost like a beautifully choreographed dance. All this in preparation of the evening dinner for her large family. I sat there constantly looking up to see if she had turned around to notice me, but all I could see was her back and glimpses of her face.

I wept silently, but hoped that it was loud enough for

her to hear. I wanted her to turn around and notice me. I wanted her to turn around and ask me what I was doing and show her pride at my scribble art. I longed to feel her arms around me. I wanted to feel the loving warmth of her body against mine. I wanted to cuddle on her lap. I wanted to hear the words, "I love you!" I wanted to know her and I wanted her to know me.

It didn't happen.

At the end of the day when she was satisfied that all her work was done, she would take off her housecoat and lay it across the bed. I'd watch her, and when she walked out of the room, I would take it and sneak it into my room where I held it tightly against my body. It didn't matter that the smell of food mingled with her sweet smell—it smelled like Mama. With tears in my eyes, I'd fall asleep, at last hugging Mama.

In hindsight, I know now that my mother was loving me—loving us—through all the things she did for us daily. She had a very large family to feed and clothe and look after, which she did so faithfully every day. She took care of us. Even though I'm sure she felt tired and frustrated, she never skipped a beat and was there for us through our childhood and adulthood. Mama was always taking care of all of us.

As I remembered this from my childhood, I thought about how many times as children of God we feel as if God isn't noticing us. We feel as if He doesn't know or understand us. We long for a turnaround. We want Him to see our tears. We want Him to see our scribbles! We fall asleep clutching His promises close to our hearts.

David—the man after God's own heart—felt that way many times. God had shown up when David killed the lion with his bare hands, confronted Goliath and won many battles. Yet there were many times in his life where he felt alone, surrounded by his enemies. David wondered if God would turn around for him. In Psalm 13:1 David asks, *"How long will you forget me, Lord? Forever? How long will you look the other way when I am in need?"* (TLB).

So, it is with us. God has been working all along in our lives, taking care of us daily. Yet in those times when He seems silent and distant, we wonder if He cares. We wonder if He hears us. We wonder if He loves us. God is there all along, but when going through difficult situations, the noise of our questions and doubts don't allow us to see and hear Him.

You may be going through a time of questioning; a time of wondering; but He assures us many times in His word that He will be there for us. Zephaniah 3:17 says, *"For the LORD your God is living among you. He is a mighty savior. He will take delight in you with gladness. With His love, He will calm all your fears. He will rejoice over you with joyful songs"* (NLT). Psalm 145 tells us that the Lord is near to all who call on Him.

My mother may not have turned around right then and there, but she was definitely aware of my presence. Later on in life as an adult, I was able to sit on her lap, give her kisses and see a big grin on her face. Her lap was a lot smaller than it had been when I was a child, but no matter if I was barely sitting on it, I was able to do it before she went from this life to glory.

God knows where you are. He will always turn around for you. You don't have to wonder. You don't have to wait. You can sit with Him right now and enjoy the beauty of His presence.

Chapter 4:
A Walk With Father

• • ● • ● • ● • ● • ● • ● • ●

Walk alongside me, Daddy
And hold my little hand.
I have so many things to learn
That I don't yet understand.

Teach me things to keep me safe
From dangers every day.
Show me how to do my best
At home, at school, at play.

Every child needs a gentle hand
To guide them as they grow.
So walk alongside me, Daddy –
We have a long way to go.

~ Helen Bush

MY FATHER AND MOTHER NEVER LEARNED TO DRIVE A CAR. They didn't feel the need to drive since rapid transit was readily available in a big city like Chicago. Most of the time, someone from the church we attended would come with a station wagon or the church bus to pick all 14 of us up, but on very rare occasions we walked. I have a treasured memory of that one rare occasion when Dad and I took that walk.

It was one very cold, dark Chicago evening. The recent snowfall had hardened to form slippery ice, but Dad decided the cold, icy conditions would not stop him from going to church. I asked if I could walk with him and waited with great anticipation for his reply. I leaped for joy when he said, "Yes." And so, we set out to walk the seven blocks to church. Seven blocks may not seem like a long way to walk, but it was to a 7-year-old like me. Even if it had been one block with my dad, I would have been just as happy.

The first thing I did was reach for his hand. It was rough but warm. I was not properly dressed for the cold. I wore a coat, a dress and my favorite pink shoes with little heels and long socks. It was a dark, blustery evening, but I hardly noticed as I was so excited to have a long evening walk with my hand in my daddy's hand.

The snow crackled under our feet and the cold wind whipped against my cheeks, but my heart was skipping as I held my father's hand, all the while trying not to slip on the ice. The warmth and happiness I felt about walking with my father—just the two of us—could have melted mounds of snow away. I felt comfort in knowing that my dad was there to keep me steady.

That night was the only time that I had my dad all to myself. Usually, we packed into a station wagon or the church bus. Sometimes, I had to sit on a sibling's lap in order to free up a seat—but not tonight. Tonight, I had him all to myself. It is a night I will always treasure in my heart. We spoke no words but no words were needed. I had all his attention, and that spoke volumes to me. I felt calm and assured that while he was with me, I would be alright.

Our walk back home was just as wonderful. I cherished it.

I may have only walked once with my hand in my earthly father's hand but I rejoice in the knowledge that I walk holding my heavenly father's hand every day of my life.

Your experience might have been different. Perhaps you never had that one moment with your father. Perhaps he wasn't around when you were growing up and you were left longing for those hands. It might be that for years you have yearned for that hand, that touch, that one moment with your father. Perhaps he walked away or was emotionally absent, leaving you with thoughts of your father that evoke feelings of bitterness.

I pray you will take comfort in the word of God that says, *"Don't be afraid, for the Lord will go before you and will be with you; He will not fail you nor forsake you"* (Deut 31:8 MSG). He is stretching out His hand to you as once again His word says, *"For even if my father and mother should abandon me, you would welcome and comfort me"* (Ps 27:10 TLB).

God is with you, not just for one night, but all the days of your life. Even when we walk through the winter of our lives and we face difficult situations, we are assured in

Psalm 23:4, *"Even when walking through the dark valley of death I will not be afraid, for You are close beside me, guarding me, guiding me all the way"* (TLB). In Matthew 28:20, He assures us that He will be with us until the end of time.

When we slip and slide through those rough roads in life; when the winds of adversity whip against us; the hand of our loving father sustains us and helps us to walk on solid ground.

The memory of that one cold night is hidden safely in my heart. The one night we walked hand in hand is etched in my memory.

Our heavenly father has extended His hand to you. If you reach out to Him, He will hold you steady. He will walk with you.

Will you walk with Him?

Chapter 5: Echoes of the Heart

· · · · · · · · · · · · · ·

"Sing and make music from your heart to the Lord"
~ *Eph 5:19b (NIV)*

OSES ARE RED MY LOVE, VIOLETS ARE BLUE, SUGAR IS SWEET MY LOVE BUT NOT AS SWEET AS YOU." The words to that song bounced on the walls and echoed up the stairwell of the three-story building on Addison and Freemont where our family lived. My sister, Carmen, and I would sit on the steps of the hallway and sing out loud, listening as our voices bounced around from wall to wall then met and danced all the way up the stairwell and came right back down to us. It was a cold, dark hallway. There was nothing special about it. There were black and white tiles at the entrance and the steps had no carpet, but oh, that echo! That made it super special to us.

Sometimes we would sit on the steps and sing in perfect harmony with our eyes closed only to open them and find our neighbors peering through their doors or looking over the banister at us. We smiled sheepishly and hoped they were grateful listeners. Their enthusiastic applause calmed any fear or doubt we had. I even think it was a welcome sound in the otherwise cold and dreary hallway. Their apparent approval only fueled our desire to do it over and over again. This was our stage, our arena. We both loved to sing, for music was what God had placed in our hearts. We sat and sang in our arena, our special place all the years we lived there. Of course, that wasn't the only song we sang but this one just lent itself for such beautiful harmony. Our parents often said they weren't sure where our talent came from. Mom could hold a tune and so could Dad, but they didn't consider themselves musically talented by any stretch of the imagination.

Our family attended a small Spanish church in the city of Chicago. As far back as I remember, we were very active in church and most Sundays, Carmen and I would sing our favorite church songs. Early in our teenage years, lyrics to what became very well-known songs were born.

We sat in our room feverishly writing song after song. I was only 15 when I wrote *Dame Fe* (Give me Faith). Later on, that song became part of the playlist in one of our recordings. We had a desire that echoed in our hearts; a desire to use our God-given talent to bring words of encouragement to all who would listen. We had absolutely no thought of fame or notoriety, only a song in our heart. Philippians 2:13 says, *"For it is God who works in you to will and to act in order to fulfill His good purpose"* (NIV). There was a purpose in our desire and God knew it. He placed it there.

In 1970, our small store front church was visited by

A WALK WITH FATHER

Sister Gwen, the president and founder of the End-time Handmaidens and Servants international. God had a purpose in sending her to our church that Sunday evening. As usual, my sister Carmen and I sang. Sister Gwen was moved to call us forward and after speaking some words over us, she prayed that God would open doors and use us. Little did we know that the gentleman accompanying her that evening, Tito Atiles, was the coordinator for an evangelistic ministry called *Cristo Viene* (Christ is Coming). This ministry was headed by Evangelist Yiye Avila. After hearing us sing, he asked us if we would be guest singers for an upcoming city-wide outreach, the first in the Chicago area for this ministry. Two small girls who thought their voices only echoed up the three-story building where they lived were now going to share a big stage. Things were about to change in a very big way.

Yiye Avila was new to Chicago. We had never heard of him, but through the coordination efforts of Tito Atiles, many pastors in Chicago and surrounding areas were going to attend along with their churches. It was an exciting time for all.

We were introduced to *Trio Melodico Congregacional*, a trio that would be in charge of playing for us during the outreach. There were no performance tapes at that time — everything was live. We waited with anticipation for the day to arrive.

It was the summer of 1970. The event took place at the First Baptist Congregational Church on Ashland Boulevard. It was a very large beautiful building with white stones and a tall steeple. It looked so majestic! We were used to our small corner of the world. This was massive! When we arrived, I felt nervous at the sight of so many cars and people lining the entrance. Inside there were many already seated. The church was full to capacity. Why us? I wondered. Why did God smile down on us this way? At this point, the evangelist hadn't even heard us sing! The audience seemed to receive us very well, but would Yiye?

After the first day, Tito Atiles told us Yiye Avila wanted to speak with our parents. We were so nervous. What was it about? He asked if they would allow us to do a professional recording for his ministry! We did, and as the old cliché says, the rest is history. We recorded not only one but three, titled, *Medico Divino*, (Divine Healer) *Grandezas de Dios*, (Greatness of God) and *Cantico Nuevo* (New Song). We went on to sing at many concerts, conferences and other church events. We were frequent guest singers at a local radio program called *Luz en el Camino* (Light in My Path), that required us to be at the station at 5 a.m.! We were teenagers—we wanted to sleep! Nonetheless, we did it. Luckily for us, it was only on Sundays.

After many years, I recorded three more albums as a soloist, *Su Voluntad* (His Will), *Sonrie* (Smile) and *¿Quien Dijo?* (Who said?). God allowed me to travel echoing the message of His love everywhere I went. He allowed me to host a radio program with my sister, Reina Sosa, and I also hosted *Hablando con Judy* (Talking with Judy), a T.V. show

A WALK WITH FATHER

in Orlando, Florida.

From one sincere echo—from one deep desire to do God's will—many doors opened up for me. It is so true that when you use the gifts He places in your hands, He will give you more and more. He allowed me to write and produce musicals and now write the book I've had in my heart to write. I had the privilege of sharing the stage with so many wonderfully talented singers and musicians throughout the years. I am thankful to many of them who embraced me and became part of my story by always being so willing to help me along. There was a particular pastor from Indiana who graciously opened up doors for me to sing for the "Year of the Hispanics" event in Anderson, Indiana—an event where singers like Larnelle Harris, Sandi Patty, The Gaithers and others were also singing. Later, I was invited to sing for the National Religious Convention in Washington, D.C.

I share this not to boast, for this is God's doing and I know that full well. But I hope to encourage you not to let anyone or anything stop you from doing what God has placed in your hands and heart to do. It wasn't easy for me. There were many stumbling stones. Only by God's grace and strength in and through me was I able to walk through the doors He opened.

What is the song or desire that echoes in your heart? Don't let it stay in the hallway of your life. Trust the One who put that desire in you. He will see you through. He will do far greater things than you can imagine.

Remember what Paul said in Galatians 6:9, *"Let us not become weary in doing good, for at the proper time we will reap a harvest if we do not give up"* (NIV). Don't give up on the song that echoes in your heart.

My Father—A Changed Man

Father & I

My Favorite Pink Shoes

Sitting on Mama's Lap

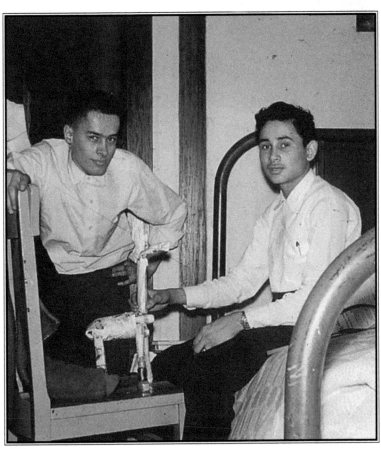

Clarence & Octavio

First Day of Crusade — 1970

With My Sister, Carmen

Doing What I Love Most...Using My Gifts

Television Show I Hosted

Stageplays

My Wonderful Husband,
Edwin

Christmas Play—2010

Chapter 6:
It is Well With My Soul

● ● ● ● ● ● ● ● ● ● ● ●

"If you are in the midst of an excruciating season of life,
I have a sure word for you. Hold on! The Lord is not finished
with you. You may think you are alone in this predicament but
all along God has been storing blessings for you that you never
dreamed of. As Peter states, His glory is going to be revealed
through your trial."
~ Gary Wilkerson

*I*T IS WELL WITH MY SOUL IS A BEAUTIFUL OLD HYMN
WRITTEN BY HORATIO SPAFFORD. It is one of my favorite hymns, but the story of how this song came to be is one of great tragedy, pain and loss.

Horatio Spafford lived in Chicago with his wife Anna, their four daughters and a son. He owned properties and was a prominent lawyer. Tragedy struck his family when his 4-year-old son died of scarlet fever. Then, in the great Chicago fire, he lost his business and all his properties. When his wife, Anna, became ill due to the stress, the doctor suggested they take a vacation. Horatio bought passage for England to travel with his family. However, unexpected business developments kept him from boarding with them. He was to follow as soon as he was able.

In November of 1873, his wife and daughters boarded the S.S. Ville du Havre, but a week into their voyage tragedy struck again. The ship collided with a powerful, iron-hulled Scottish ship, the Loch Earn. The S.S. Ville du Havre sank quickly. Over 200 souls lost their lives, including Horatio's four daughters. Only his wife survived.

As soon as Anna was able, she sent a message to her husband letting him know the tragic news. Horatio bought passage to be by her side. I can't imagine how he felt. What were his thoughts as he traveled over the same waters that took his daughters lives? It is said that the ship's captain pointed out to Horatio the very spot where the ship carrying his family had sunk. It was an unimaginable tragedy. Yet from all of this, Horatio penned the song that has been a source of peace and hope for so many, "It is Well With My Soul." How could anyone say such words in light of all that had happened? Hadn't he lost his business, his properties, his son and now his daughters?

1982 was a very hard year for me; one which threw me into a time of deep sadness and depression. Although I dare not compare my pain with that of Horatio Spafford, I, too, penned a song that was birthed through great pain but became a source of peace and hope.

At the age of 27 I had my second child. It should have been a time of great joy for me, my baby and my husband, but it wasn't. My marriage was ending. I was hit by a vessel,

46

not one made of iron or steel, but nonetheless it hit with such force it sent a deep piercing pain all over my body, soul and mind. The striking vessel was called, divorce! It was a tearing of the soul, a wrenching pain that threw me "overboard." It was the severing of two people who had vowed at the altar, "...'Til death do us part." Death came, but not the kind that puts you in a coffin and where people gather to cry and say sweet things about you. It was death to a life you planned; death to celebrating anniversaries and growing old together. I felt as if divorce was now tattooed on my forehead and I carried this label with shame.

At the time, I was a very well-known Spanish Christian singer. I shuddered at the thought of what people would think and say about me. I rolled up in a fetal position and cried. I sat in a dark room. Only the darkness of the room matched what I felt inside.

As I cried and spoke to the Lord, I was drawn to the book of Psalms and began to cry out as David had. David was very bold in expressing his feelings to God, even questioning him as in Psalm 10:1, *"Lord, why are you standing aloof and away? Why do you hide when I need you the most?"* Every day on my knees I read Psalms in prayer and it was as though my tears mingled with David's. God definitely heard and answered David. Would He do it for me too?

I spoke about my feelings to no one and I think people didn't dare to invade my space and try to reach me. I was living upstairs in the three-story apartment building my sister and her husband owned, but I felt very alone. It isn't always easy to give words of comfort to someone who has gone through a loss of any kind. I wasn't approached and I didn't approach anyone either. It was just me and my Lord.

I was working at a hospital as an Outpatient Registrar but had taken some time off. When the time came to return, I did so reluctantly. My ex-husband also worked there and seeing him would be another blow that I could not bear. Time passed and I kept my routine of going to work, going home, getting on my knees and reading Psalms in prayer. This went on for several months.

One day, as I registered a patient into the clinic, I started hearing beautiful voices singing. It was as though the voices fell into my ears like rain. It's hard to explain but that's how it felt. The message of those words was familiar to me. They were words spoken to Job as he laid on his sick bed. For months, he not only suffered the pain of losing his children but the physical pain of having his body covered in boils. His friends who came over to "console" him only made matters worse. The accusations and assumptions hurled at him were like pouring alcohol on the sores on his body. As Christians, we should be careful not to feel so smug about our "standing" with the Lord. When we do, we become like Job's friends and instead of helping, we doubt and accuse.

Job's pain was great and his "comforters" only made it worse, which fueled Job to defend himself (Job 15). God lets him go on with his defense but in Job 38, God begins asking him questions which Job could not answer. "Where

When I got home after work, I wrote the words down and asked God to help me finish making them into a song. Finally, I felt excited about something. I'd like to share the lyrics to that song. They are translated from Spanish:

The sun lost its shine
Rain was unceasing
And I didn't understand why
I wanted to see a rainbow appear
I wanted everything to fall into place
Yes, there was a time in my life where I found myself in turmoil
I didn't understand why, I felt alone and abandoned
And I saw no way out
But one day I heard the voice as many voices sang to me this way
Where were you when I made the heavens
Where were you when I made the seas
I am Jehovah, I am Alpha and Omega
What I did yesterday I can also do today
And in the fields tell me who dresses the lilies?
Not even Solomon dressed as one of these
Who feeds the birds of the air?

A WALK WITH FATHER

Fear not for I do all these things
He also said in his word
And who by worrying can add a single moment to their life?
And why worry about what to wear?
Consider the lilies of the fields they neither labor nor spin
But I tell you that not even Solomon dressed as one of these
And if the grass of the field that is here today
And tomorrow is tossed
Into the fire and still
God dresses them like this
Won't He do the same for you oh ye of little faith?
But seek first the kingdom of God and all else will be added unto
you.
Suddenly a great peace came over me
Because I realized there really is no need to worry
We simply need to trust our lives into the hands of the Lord

About three years after I wrote this song, I recorded it and received many testimonies of how it was a source of great blessing and peace. The song was requested often on Chicago's Moody Radio Spanish station. One testimony I received was from a pastor. She told me of a lady in her church that had lost a child and had sunken into depression. The pastor visited her one day and told her, "I am not going to say anything I just want you to listen to this." She played the song for her. The lady wept as those words showered into her mind and soul bringing peace and calm. God reminded her—as He had done to me—that He was there. He knew. He saw and He cared. She later testified how the message of that song had helped her come out of her depression. I treasure letters I received from strangers who wrote to share their words of gratitude at being blessed by the song.

Pain is a process we all go through. It's almost impossible not to feel pain when things fall apart. The pain of the breakup of a marriage, the loss of a loved one or like in the case of Horatio and Job, the loss of all they owned and even their beloved children can be unbearable. What we do with our pain determines where we will end up.

I know of women who lost their will and their way because of divorce. Ravaged by the pain, they turned to alcohol and drugs for comfort. That could have been me if not for the grace of my Lord. I had a choice—to abandon myself to depression, or abandon myself in the arms of the Lord. I thank God He helped me choose the latter. I can't say I was perfect during that time. I made several bad judgements along the way but I thank God that He looked past my imperfections and saw my pain. It's so good to know that God remembers that we are but dust (Ps 103:14) and has mercy. He understands that we are limited but His mercy is limitless. He raised me from the dust and put my feet on solid ground.

Years have passed since I "walked through the valley of the shadow of death" as David would put it (Ps 23). God reminded me who He was. God reminded me that He is *able to do immeasurably more than all we ask or imagine, according to His power that is at work within us* (Eph 3:20 NIV).

And so, I thank God that in the end I have been able to sing, "It is well, it is well, with my soul!" For surely, He has blessed me beyond measure, definitely beyond what I deserve. He turned my mourning into gladness. He turned my ashes into beauty.

He is so willing to do the same for you. He can piece the fragments of your tattered and torn life and cause you to sing—indeed, "It is well with my soul."

Chapter 7:
He Turned it Around

● ● ● ● ● ● ● ● ● ● ●

"In you they trusted and were not disappointed."
~ Ps 22:5b (NASB)

HAVE YOU EVER HAD SOMEONE TRY TO PULL THE RUG OUT FROM UNDER YOU? Or you were sailing along when all of a sudden someone stands up on your boat and intentionally starts rocking it, trying to make you fall? You don't know why it is happening and no reasoning gets the person to sit down.

Such was the case with me.

I awaited with great anticipation for a call from a very prestigious company. One might have thought I was crazy to apply at a company that only hired people with advanced degrees—something I did not have—but when I learned about an opening, I applied anyway. I prayed and trusted God would come through.

At the time, I was a single mom living with my oldest sister and her family. I needed this job in order to settle in a place of my own with my two daughters.

My sister was very gracious and accommodating, but I

still had financial responsibilities. I needed to be financially independent. My sister had done enough; opening up her home and letting us stay as long as necessary.

I had seen God move on my behalf on so many occasions. Once, I had to take care of a financial obligation that was due the next day, but I didn't have the money. I didn't want my sister to know. She would have insisted on helping me and I didn't want to burden her. That night, I prayed and cried before the Lord, asking for His intervention.

The next morning, there was a knock at the door. I heard my sister speaking with someone, but couldn't make out what they were saying. The sound of the front door closing was followed by a knock on my bedroom door. My sister handed me a small envelope and said, "Jenna (name changed) asked me to give you this. She said God spoke to her and told her to do this."

I was curious. What could it be? When I opened the envelope, three crisp $100 bills fell out! God came through at the precise time of need.

I was confident I would get the call from the company to which I applied, and sure enough I did. God opened the door for me to walk into my blessing. I was hired to work in the Payroll department as a payroll representative. I was ecstatic!

A year and a half later, I saw a posting for a position in the Human Resources department. I took my chances, applied and was hired. Everything was going smoothly, but around my seventh month in that department, my supervisor called me in to her office. What she told me hit me like a big bucket of ice water! She said she was not satisfied with my work and was giving me a month to find another position within the company or I would be out of a job. What? She had not complained before. She seemed to be satisfied. There were no reports of any wrongdoing or complaints from other departments. What happened?

I cried all the way home. I went before the Lord in tears. "How Lord?" I cried. "Wasn't it You who opened this door for me? How can someone just come and slam it shut in my face?"

I lost sleep thinking about what I should do. I felt very strongly that I should speak to my supervisor about the whole matter, but I just wasn't a bold enough person.

I have always been quiet and shy, so the next day when I walked into the Human Resources department, I felt extremely nervous. I was shaking like a leaf. The urge to go speak with her grew stronger and stronger. I was breathing so hard I could have passed out from hyperventilating. Even in my hesitation, I felt as if these large, invisible hands were pushing me towards her office while I stepped on the brakes all the way there. What would she think? What would she say?

Once in the office she motioned for me to sit down. I know it was by the prompting of the Spirit that I found the courage to speak these words through my tears. "I don't know why you are doing this to me but I want you to know the word of God assures me that He works all things out

for my good. All this is going to turn around for my good!"
I said boldly. Did I say that? Was that even me speaking? I
even did a circle with my finger as I pointed at her.

She was stunned and her mouth just hung open. The
only thing she said was, "I hope so, Honey." With that, I
walked out of her office. I felt as if I was walking on Jell-O.
My feet were unsteady. I put out my hands trying to reach
for my chair almost as if trying to find it in the dark. I
plopped down on the chair. I did it! I spoke the words that
needed to be said and I put God in it, so now He had to
show up on my behalf. He certainly wasn't going to let His
word return void.

At night I continued to pray. As the days passed, the
ticking of the clock seemed to make fun of me! "Tick tock!
Ding dong! A few more days and you'll be gone!"

Daily I scanned through the list of job openings but
nothing. Oh, there were openings alright but mostly for
high level positions for which I did not qualify.

One day, a new hire came into the office. She had recently started as a temporary worker for the Accounts
Receivables department. She had done so well that they
decided to hire her before the time of eligibility for perma-
nent employment was up. I helped her fill out the new hire
paperwork and heard how they were singing her praises.

I had two weeks left to find a job. As I searched the
job postings, still I saw nothing. Our human tendency is to
grow desperate when things aren't moving fast enough. We
start doubting if indeed we made the right moves or said

the right things. Was I wrong to tell my supervisor what I told her? We have to be careful not to let words of doubt and fear escape our lips. I had opened my mouth to declare what I knew from God's word and what I felt He was saying about the situation.

Little did I know, the lady who had been recently hired in Accounts Receivables—the one they sang praises about—suddenly started accusing her co-workers of sabotaging her work. One day, she became so angry, she lost it and stormed out! Now that position became available and I applied. Just a few short days after my interview and before doomsday, I was hired. And let me tell you, it wasn't just another position. Oh no, it was a grade higher and with that came higher pay! In essence, it was a promotion.

I actually think God had her there just to hold that position for me. You see, the manager of the Accounts Receivables department had previously been the assistant manager in the Payroll department where I worked. He had recently moved into his new position. Coincidental? He knew me and my work ethics. I feel sure that even if a more qualified applicant had applied, God would have held that door open for me! I had declared with my mouth and believed in my heart that He would turn the situation around for my good.

As I later found out, my supervisor tried to pull the rug from under me because her plans were to give my position to a friend of hers. She never mentioned our conversation when she signed my transfer paper to my new department, but weeks later I heard she had become ill and had to leave her position.

God had it all under control. From the moment He urged me to speak in faith, those words opened up a whole new door for me. I just couldn't see it yet. After things fall into place and we see the handiwork of God, we marvel at how God had it laid out all the time. We are amazed by how He moves things around just like pieces on a chess board (Rom 8:28). How marvelous are His works!

Perhaps someone may be trying to pull the rug out from under you. Someone might be "rocking your boat" and trying to make your life miserable. You may feel tempted to fight in your own strength or storm out and quit. But if you open your mouth in faith declaring what the word of God says, He will open a new and better door for you. I've seen this over and over again.

Sometimes a "Goliath" comes to defy you and your faith. The situation seems insurmountable. But when we exult the name of the Lord and speak words of faith, it's like hurling stones that are precise and hit the enemy straight on. Proverbs 18:21 tells us *"The power of life and death are in the tongue."* We can shoot down the enemy with words of faith or we can shoot ourselves in the foot by speaking defeat.

Trust God to turn it around. He can do it!

Chapter 8:
Pulling on the Wrong Door

● ● ● ● ● ● ● ● ● ● ● ●

"I was looking for the keys for years
but the door was always open."
~ *Aravind Adiga*

THE LUCILLE BALL SHOW FIRST AIRED IN OCTOBER OF 1962 AND QUICKLY BECAME ONE OF AMERICA'S MOST LOVED SHOWS. Who couldn't love that crazy redhead who caused so much mayhem, always guaranteeing a great belly laugh? Like the time she baked a loaf of bread that came out of the oven so huge that it knocked her into the living room! The one I like best is when she and Ethel, her sidekick, were working at a chocolate factory and had to wrap chocolate candy as it came down a conveyer belt. The supervisor had warned them that if one candy got through without being wrapped, they'd be fired. The job seemed easy enough. At first, the candies came through and they had no problem, but all of a sudden, the belt sped up. They tried and tried to wrap every single candy but were not able to keep up. In order to conceal the candies they couldn't wrap, they began to stuff their mouths and even their clothes with them! The faster the belt went, the more they had to stuff. Hilarious! Even with all her best intentions, Lucy always had a knack of messing things up and getting herself into some predicament.

Well, I've done quite a few "Lucy's" in my life. Yes, I'm ashamed to admit it but I have. One of my Lucy's happened when I was at home with a new puppy I was training. After doing a few things around the house I took my sweet little pup named Sassy into my arms and opened the door to let her out so she could run around and get used to the backyard. I was out there for about 15 minutes and decided it was time to go back in. I picked up my puppy and then pulled on the back door. It wouldn't open. The door was locked! I panicked. I pulled and pulled and even looked through the window as if that was going to help. No one was home. My husband, Edwin, was at work. "Oh my God," I thought. "Now what am I going to do?"

It was October and it was already a bit chilly and I wasn't wearing a sweater. I went over and over in my mind wondering how this happened. I decided to go to my neighbor's house and ask to use her phone to call my husband. Almost in hysteria I explained, "I went out to take Sassy and the door locked on me! I don't know what to do. It's cold and I can't get back in!" My husband was a little confused. How could I get locked out? Our doors were not self-locking. Anyway, he said he'd try to leave work as soon as possible.

I sat outside waiting for my husband to come. He was

working about 3o minutes away from our home, which seemed like an eternity to me. I was sitting on our swing shivering while I held my puppy tight.

After a while, my husband opened the back door from inside the house and said, "I don't understand how you got locked out. The door is unlocked!"

I looked at him quite befuddled and asked, "How could that be? I pulled and pulled and the door wouldn't open! Then how did I get locked out?" He took me around to the front of the house to show me the front door was open. It was open all along. I had gone out through the front door but when trying to get back in I had convinced myself I had actually gone out the back door! "Lucy, you have some 'splaining to do!!!" I was pulling and pulling on the wrong door. Luckily, my husband has a great sense of humor and we have been laughing about this ever since.

The door incident made me think of how often we convince ourselves that we are "locked out" in life. We pull and pull. We try this and that and nothing happens! The door is locked and there is no way in. What we fail to realize is that we are pulling on the wrong door. At times, we try to involve others to pull on that closed door for us as I had done. Have you ever stood in front of a door and you pulled and pulled trying to get it to open, only to realize there is a sign you overlooked that says, PUSH? It happens more often than we realize.

When we find ourselves in front of a door we can't open then we start assuming. My assumption convinced me that the door I was pulling was the correct one, when in fact, it wasn't. We jump to conclusions. Our minds race and many times we end up getting into the wrong place, not the place God had intended.

Doing a "Lucy" as I had done was funny, but insisting on pulling on the wrong door can get us into a heap of trouble. We pull and pull. We force it open. You insisted on a certain job, location, house, or marriage only to realize it was absolutely wrong for you. Many times, we just have to wait on the right time for that door to open.

I've gone several times to a store and pulled on the door but it was closed. That door was going to open and allow me in but I had to wait. There was a set time for that door to open. So it is in life. It could be the wrong door or the wrong time. In my case, it was the wrong door because the right one was open. I just didn't realize it or even make an attempt to see if maybe the other door was open.

If you find that you have been pulling and pulling on a door that just doesn't seem to open, ask yourself if perhaps you are pulling on the wrong door. Alexander Graham Bell once said, "When one door closes another one opens; but we often look so long and so regretfully upon the closed door, that we do not see the one which has opened for us."

Don't look at or to the closed door. Instead, ask God to show you which door He has for you to walk through. Pray and seek guidance (Prov 15:22). Let His word be the light, the lamp that guides your feet in the right direction (Ps 119:105). God will take you by the hand and show you the right door, the right time and the door of blessing that was open for you all along.

Chapter 9:
Love Keeps No Record of Wrong

• • • • • • • • • • •

"We can't receive today's joys while holding
on to yesterday's sadness."
~ Judy Mendez Martinez

I'VE BEEN KEEPING A DIARY SINCE EARLY 70'S. When I
was younger, I was extremely shy about having con-
versations with anyone, and pretty much kept to myself. I
was and still am an introvert. In fact, I was so shy that when
I started school, I was assigned an interpreter because the
teacher thought I didn't speak or understand English.

After watching the movie, "The Diary of Anne Frank" I
got the idea that I too should have a "Kitty," a dairy. I didn't
have an actual diary like Anne did so I started mine in a
small black notebook. A diary for me was a solution to having someone to "tell" things to. I wrote about things going
on at home, school and boys I liked. Now I had somewhere
to pour out my feelings openly without fear of rejection,
reproach or judgement. I always had a love for writing and
this diary afforded me the opportunity to write my life's
stories and poems.

For a while, my diary sat untouched in my dresser drawer until a situation occurred that hurt me very much. I am not and have never been a confrontational person. Since I hate conflicts, my first thought was to get out my diary and go to task recounting how hurt I felt at what had just happened. I wanted to write every single little detail so that when I died and the diary was read, that person would be (I hoped anyway) very remorseful and as hurt as I had been. I wanted the words written in my diary to say, "Yeah you did that. Aren't you ashamed?" Yes, our flesh eggs us on insisting, "Do it. They deserve it. Boy, will they be sorry!"

With those feelings in my heart, I readied myself with pen in hand, nose flared, tears running down my cheeks to write what I thought needed to be said. My shaky hand headed for the paper when I heard an inner voice tell me, *"Love keeps no record of wrongs!"* (1 Cor 13:5d NIV). My first thought was, "What? Aw, come on, not now! Don't remind me of that now! You were there. You saw. You know I need to let all of this out!" An arm wrestle ensued. My desire to vent and God's word were doing battle in my spirit. Thankfully the Word won. Later, when I calmed down, I realized my words were going to do more harm than good and I pictured the hurt I would cause someone at a time when apologies would no longer matter.

It doesn't come easy for us to stay silent, to walk away and especially forgive. By keeping a record, we allow for those feelings to stay alive festering and sizzling like Al-ka-Seltzer in our soul, causing emotional and physical harm. Opening up to read what we wrote at a time of anger and hurt could only give rise to those feelings as if it was a fresh incident. We read it, rehashing and rehearsing every word, bringing up tears and resentment.

With the passing of time, I was able to speak to that person—not all at once but slowly and piece by piece as the occasion allowed—now in a calmer manner. If you are of that nature where you can sit with someone who has hurt you and can have that conversation right away, I suggest you do. Resolve it so you won't have it stored in your heart or written anywhere to surface later and cause more harm.

God's Word says in 1 Corinthians 13:4-7, *"Love is patient, love is kind. It does not envy, it does not boast, it is not proud. It does not dishonor others, it is not self-seeking, it is not easily angered, it keeps no record of wrongs. Love does not delight in evil but rejoices with the truth. It always protects, always trusts, always hopes, always perseveres"* (NIV).

If we don't do this, we will never be able to enjoy the freedom forgiveness brings. We can't enjoy the beauty of today when our life is held with a ball and chain to events that no longer exist.

Chapter 10:
Family: A Gift from God

• • • • • • • • • • • •

"The love of family is like the roots of an oak tree.
The deeper the roots; the stronger the foundation."
~ *Vickie Lynell Evans*

I HAVE FOUR GRANDCHILDREN, MY "COCONUTS" AS I CALL
THEM. There is Alexis Rose, my first beautiful co-
conut, then Jordan Anthony, my handsome young man,
Jae Lynn, beautiful and sweet, and then there is Sofia, my
beautiful rock star grandbaby! She is our little chatter box
with old soul. She sits with her legs crossed as she whisks
her hair to the side in her adult stance as she chatters on
and on.

Sofia and my husband, Edwin, whom the grands call
"Wuelo" (short for *abuelo*, which is "grandfather" in Spanish), have a love-hate relationship. Well, not really hate but
you know what I mean.

Edwin loves to tease and if he sees that it bothers you,
he does it more, in jest, of course. When our daughter, Jenny, was young, he would scrunch up a pillow and snuggle
on it making smacking sounds with his lips. For some rea-

son that really bothered Jenny and she'd come calling on me to have him stop. He still does it whenever he sees her and gets the same reaction! To Alexis, he rolls his shoulders as he looks to the side. But Sofia, oh Sofia, he really enjoys getting her all riled up. She will not have it and so they go on and on about silly things like, "Is E.T. real?" Edwin tells her that E.T. is his friend. At first she'd say, "He's not real. He's only a movie!" with her eyebrows frowned and her little finger pointing at him. But somehow Edwin convinced her that indeed E.T. is his friend. Even though Edwin teases her, every time she comes for a visit, the first thing she does when she walks through the door is ask, "Where's Wuelo?" Too sweet.

Alexis was only two years old when she and her mom came to live with us here in North Carolina. She was the apple of my eye. When she cried, I would rock her in my arms and sing lullabies as she stared intently at me. We'd play hide and seek for hours or she would get on a throw and I would pull her 'round and 'round on the floor. Jordan and Jae Lynn live in another state and although I've had great times with them, I haven't had as much time as I wish to. To them I was the "tickle monster!" I'd tickle them until they dropped on the floor, but they always came back for more. God is so awesome to let us enjoy our children and then our grandchildren.

It is a gift to be able to look at our children and our grandchildren and see the wonder of God. A family unit is such a beautiful thing. I admire families that are able to get along well and share many wonderful moments together, laughing, crying or joking as they create beautiful memories. There are family outings, family dinners, weddings and holidays to enjoy and keep in the treasure boxes of our minds.

I have an actual box where I store all the cards and notes I received through the years from my girls and coconuts. I also have some toys, socks and security blankets. Every time I open the box to add something or just look through everything, I remember the feeling of being a new mom and grandmama. Time passes, memories don't.

Family is a very important unit created by God. When God chose to reveal Himself, He did so through family. He could have very well just shown up and said, "I am here. I am God." But He didn't. As Christians, our families should reflect God and His love. We may have moments of disagreement and rivalry, even times of being apart due to misunderstandings.

In the story of the prodigal son in Luke 15, we see a vivid picture of God and family dynamics. I'm sure the prodigal son enjoyed many great moments in his home. He had everything he needed and lacked for no good thing, but just like our children or grandchildren often do, he chose another way. The story of the prodigal son is a picture of God the Father waiting with open arms for all those who have strayed to come back to Him. It is also a picture of forgiveness as it pertains to our families.

Our children may stray away from the home and even

from the Lord, but look at what Luke 15:17-20 says. *"When he came to his senses, he said, 'How many of my father's hired servants have food to spare, and here I am starving to death! I will set out and go back to my father and say to him: Father, I have sinned against heaven and against you. I am no longer worthy to be called your son; make me like one of your hired servants.' So, he got up and went to his father. But while he was still a long way off, his father saw him and was filled with compassion for him; he ran to his son, threw his arms around him and kissed him"* (NIV). While his son was still a long way off his father saw him. I can only imagine the father going out there every day longing for the day his son would return. What a beautiful picture of love and forgiveness. Is there someone you need to forgive?

Perhaps you can't say you had a loving family unit. You might be saying, "My parents weren't a gift. My siblings are definitely not a gift." You may have been raised in a very dysfunctional family and your views on family are distorted, but not all family is from our blood line. God provides family through friends, church, adoption and other means (Prov 18:24).

Recently, I saw a report on the evening news of a young boy named Jason who had lived in a group home for six years. The report said Jason wanted a sense of normalcy and the love of a parent. When asked what he wished for himself, he responded, "I would just like to have a family to call Mom and Dad, or just Mom, or just Dad. I don't really care." He just wanted a family, from his bloodline or not.

Everyone wants that. Everyone wants to be loved. Everyone wants to belong. God is our heavenly father who loves us more than our human minds can comprehend. John 3:16 says, *"For God so loved the world that He gave His only son that who so ever believes in Him shall not perish but have eternal life"* (NIV). Such is the love of Abba Father. If you haven't enjoyed the love of family, I pray that you will enjoy the fellowship and the love your heavenly God offers every day. I pray He brings people into your life whom you can call family and with whom you can make wonderful memories.

Chapter 11:
God Loves You

• • • • • • • • • • • • •

"The beloved is like breathing the freshest air,
eating the finest food, like living heaven on earth."
~ Judy Mendez Martinez

SEVERAL YEARS AGO, I WAS FEELING A BIT SAD, WON-DERING IF GOD REALLY LOVED ME. I remember crying and praying just before I went to bed and I asked him just like that, "God do you love me?" I laid down on my bed and closed my eyes. I'm not sure how much time passed but I remember feeling a small breeze like when someone comes and stands by you. I felt the warmth of a body and a hand that caressed my head for a few seconds. I opened my eyes and sat up, but there was no one there! I felt a peace come over me. I knew it was an answer to my question. It was Him saying, "Yes, Judy. I do love you!"

God loves me. God loves you. God loves us. Yes, He does. God's love is never ending. Nothing can separate us from the love of God. I love these verses in Romans 8:35-38, *"Who shall separate us from the love of Christ? Shall trouble or hardship or persecution or famine or nakedness or danger or sword? As it is written: 'For your sake we face death all day long; we are considered as sheep to be slaughtered.' No, in all these things we are more than conquerors through Him who loved us. For I am convinced that neither death nor life, neither angels nor demons, neither the present nor the future, nor any powers, neither height nor depth, nor anything else in all creation, will be able to separate us from the love of God that is in Christ Jesus our father"* (NIV). How powerful, how comforting to know that nothing can take us from His love. His love never changes, never fails, never ends.

I want to end this book by reminding you that God is able, willing and ready to hear you when you call. He says, *"When you pass through the waters, I will be with you; and when you pass through the rivers, they will not sweep over you. When you walk through the fire, you will not be burned; the flames will not set you ablaze"* (Isaiah 43:2 NIV). How wonderful are His promises! I speak from my own experience about God's faithfulness.

You may have gone through situations in your life where you wonder if He really loves you. You might be going through something even now. But I am sure there were so many things you don't realize that God kept you from. You are alive! He is inviting you to the biggest event this world has ever known. He invites you and every day He reminds you to get ready. The invitation has been sent out, Revelations 19:6b-9 reads, *"Hallelujah! For our Lord God Almighty reigns. Let us rejoice and be glad and give him glory! For the wedding of the Lamb has come, and his bride has made her-*

self ready. Fine linen, bright and clean, was given her to wear. Then the angel said to me, 'Write this: Blessed are those who are invited to the wedding supper of the Lamb!' And he added, 'These are the true words of God'" (NIV).

You have a personal invitation. You were and you are still within his reach. You still have an opportunity to ask, to seek and most importantly, R.S.V.P. to be part of the biggest celebration ever known to man. We are living in uncertain times and I invite you to find peace, rest and joy in your walk with Father.

Love you,

Judy